GEEKS CAN'T DANCE

Highfield South Farnham
Weydon Lane
Farnham
Surrey
GU9 8QH

Jo Cotterill

Illustrated by **Xavier Bonet**

OXFORD
UNIVERSITY PRESS

When I was at school, I was a geek. (Well, back then the word was 'swot'.) I wasn't part of the 'cool gang', but I had some good friends. And then, one day, those friends decided they weren't my friends any more, and they froze me out. It was horrible and I didn't know what to do. Luckily I found some new friends in the end, but it was a sad and anxious time for me.

It's sometimes hard to know how to fit in. What if you like carpentry and ballet? What if you like rugby and cooking? My advice is if you love doing something, you should do it lots, no matter what anyone thinks. That way, not only will you get really good at it, but it will make you happy too! And in the end, that's what we all want, isn't it?

Jo Cotterill
(who likes maths and pretty dresses)

Chapter 1
An Awesome Surprise

Have you heard of fractals? Fractals are *amazing*. They're patterns that repeat over and over again.

Ferns are fractals. Each leaf is made up of repeats of the same pattern, getting smaller and smaller. Some snowflakes are fractals too, repeating the same pattern over and over to their tips.

When I first heard that, I went 'WHOOAAA.' I have a poster of a fractal on my bedroom wall.

I love science. It's bonkers and brilliant. Plus, fractals make AMAZING pictures.

Next to my fractal poster, I have a poster of my favourite band, On The Up. They're all *very* dreamy.

It's Tuesday, and I'm nearly late for school because I'm listening to a podcast about radio waves. When I listen to podcasts, my walking slows down, so it isn't until my best friend Jazz shouts in my face that I realize how late it is.

'Keisha! The bell! Come on!'

Hastily, I pull my headphones out and run across the playground with her. I mean the yard. You don't call it a playground at this school. Playgrounds are for young kids. I'm at secondary school now.

Jazz and I bump and trip our way to our form room for register. There are so many people in this school. It's impossible to walk in a straight line. I start to wonder if there's a formula for finding the quickest route along a straight corridor when it's full of people. I should design an experiment to find out.

Jazz digs an elbow into me. 'Ouch!' I say.

She gives me a *look* and nods towards the front of the room.

Mr Benwell is staring at me, the register in his hand.

'Oh!' I say. 'Sorry. Here, sir!'

Mr Benwell finishes the register and then consults his notes. 'Announcements this morning,' he says. 'French with Miss Dubois won't be in Room 34. Please go to Science Lab Four instead. Er ... we're expecting a fire drill at some point today, so remember that when it sounds, you need to leave everything behind and go outside in an orderly fashion. Leave *everything* behind,' he repeats firmly, looking at Nula Tsempe. Nula won't go anywhere without her bag. It's full of make-up.

'Lastly,' Mr Benwell says, 'the Fundraising Committee is looking for more volunteers to help out. As you know, the upper years at the school get a prom in the summer, while you younger ones get a Winter Ball just before the end of term. This year the committee has booked a rather expensive band.' Mr Benwell raises his eyebrows and shakes his head. 'I have to say, we don't normally pay out this much – but I gather they're very popular. Anyway, more help is needed for the fundraising.'

People start whispering around me. I put up my hand.

'Yes, Keisha?'

'Who have they booked? I mean – which band is it?'

Mr Benwell looks down at his piece of paper again. 'Uh ... On The Up. Is that right?'

But his last words are drowned out by the whooping and cheering that breaks out. My jaw drops in astonishment. On The Up? But ... but ... they're in the charts and everything! They're in magazines and on chat shows on TV! They're *on my bedroom wall*!

Jazz grabs my arm tightly.

'We are signing up for that committee RIGHT NOW. We *have* to get the money for that band!'

My head hurts from all the nodding I'm doing.

* * *

The Fundraising Committee meets in one of the classrooms, and we can hardly get in the door at lunchtime. There are so many excited kids from our year; Jazz and I have to squeeze between them to hear what's being said.

'Here!' Chloe and Zeek wave us over, so we go and join them. Chloe is chewing her nails, which she does all the time, even though it's gross. Zeek is her boyfriend. Sort of. They hang around together, anyway. I'm not sure if that makes him her boyfriend or not. Zeek's mum is a hairdresser and he is a total fashionista. He even makes the school uniform look cool.

'Shush!' Someone is shouting at the front of the classroom. It's Jessica, from a couple of years above us. 'Be quiet!'

Jessica introduces herself as the head of the Fundraising Committee. Then she points out three other students who are organizers too. 'As you know,' she says to us all, 'we've booked On The Up for the Winter Ball.'

Cheering breaks out at this, and Jessica smiles excitedly. 'I know, I know. But they want three thousand pounds to come and perform.'

'WHAT?' exclaims Jazz, and my jaw drops for the second time that day. Three thousand pounds! That's a huge amount!

Everyone looks dismayed. How on earth were we meant to raise that kind of money in two months?

Jessica waves her arms to get attention.

'It's actually much less than they normally charge. They're doing us a special deal because Mr Hanover went to school with their manager or something.' Mr Hanover is our head teacher. 'I know it seems a lot,' Jessica continues, 'but we think we can do it. We need loads of ideas and events. Cake sales, jumble sales, bingo, raffles – whatever you can come up with. And of course, we'll need volunteers to help run the events.

'So, if you just came along today thinking you'd help blow up a few balloons on the night – there's the door.' She points at it. 'If you're here to help, that means *commitment*. Giving up your time, sacrificing some of your evenings and weekends so we can all have an amazing Winter Ball at the end of it. You've got ten seconds to decide whether you're in or out.' She folds her arms.

There's a buzz of talk and movement. Some people do head out of the door. But most people stay. Jazz and I stay, OBVIOUSLY. So do Chloe and Zeek.

'Right,' says Jessica, when everyone has settled again, 'you guys are going to get us the best dance in the history of this school. We'll be meeting again tomorrow after lessons, and I want all of you to bring an idea. Something that could actually make some cash. OK? Oh – one other thing. The band's manager says that they're happy to meet with a small group of students and pose for photos and stuff. But only a small group – not everyone who'll be at the dance. So ... ' she glances at the other members of the committee, 'we've decided that we'll make the fundraising into a competition. The group whose event makes the most money will get to meet On The Up face-to-face: up close and personal.'

I gasp, and so does pretty much everyone else in the room.

I could *meet* On The Up! I could stand right next to them! This is the most exciting thing that's EVER happened!

Chapter 2
The Competition

For the rest of the afternoon, Jazz, Chloe, Zeek and I whisper excited ideas to each other in every spare moment. We get told off quite a lot in lessons, but it's worth it because by the end of the day we have what we think is a truly brilliant idea. 'Everyone knows what they have to do this evening, don't they?' Jazz says as we part at the school gates.

I nod. I have to do some online research – vital for our idea. The others nod too. 'See you tomorrow,' Jazz says, and high fives me before heading off. I plug in my headphones, but instead of returning to my podcast, I flip through my audio library and find On The Up's album. Then I walk home, humming along and dreaming of meeting my music heroes.

* * *

When I get home, I run straight up to my room, calling out a hello to my mum who's downstairs in her study. She works from home, which is handy if I'm off sick or anything. I dump my bag on the floor and open my laptop. It's Mum's old one, which means it crashes sometimes, but it's good enough for finding stuff online.

I open a search engine and type in 'hairstyles'. It's not the kind of thing I usually look for! But for our idea we need to create a poster, and so we'll need loads of images to put into a collage.

I start saving pictures into a folder, and then something catches my eye. It's titled 'STYLISH SCIENTIST ON THE RED CARPET', and it's about a woman who works for NASA, the space agency. She's wearing a floor-length blue dress and has her hair all done up. Underneath, it says, 'Aeronautical engineer Suzi Klyser takes a day off from saving the planet.'

Aeronautical engineer. Wow. She must be super clever. I open a new window and type in her name. She has a profile on the NASA website, and she's written several articles. I start reading ...

Suzi designs satellites. She's worked on rovers too – the little machines on wheels they send to planets to gather samples and do experiments. She's been to two universities, and has lots of letters after her name for all her qualifications.

At the bottom of one of the articles, there's a box. 'WIN A TRIP TO NASA!' the headline shouts. I read on.

Open to all children aged 8–16 based in the UK. We will fly you and your family to Florida for a once-in-a-lifetime trip to the Kennedy Space Center! See a real space shuttle. Try astronaut food. And talk space, time and all the dimensions between with some of the brainiest people on the planet.

I can hardly breathe. This is like a dream come true! My hands shake. What do I have to do to win?

There are many different scientific theories that help us to understand our world. We'd like you to pick just ONE and make a short one-minute video, explaining the theory to your viewers. Maybe you'll re-enact Newton's discovery of the law of gravity by sitting underneath an apple tree? Maybe you'll demonstrate Archimedes's 'eureka' moment about water displacement in the bath! (But keep your clothes on, please!) You can explain the

theory in whatever way you think is best –
but you must upload it to our site before the
deadline.

Then we'll open the site to **viewer voting** –
that's right! The winner will be selected by YOU,
the general public. When voting closes, we'll
have our winner, and they can look forward to
the trip of a lifetime, along with a great prize
for their school!

I look up from my screen at the wall behind
it. Mingling with the posters of On The Up and
kittens are the fractals and a colourful double
helix, and a diagram explaining how light is split
through a prism. Science is everywhere, and I love
it. I love that there are theories behind everything.
It's like life is a huge complicated computer
program, and you can find out how it's made by
learning the coding language.

I *have* to enter that competition. When is the
deadline? I check, and gulp.

Three weeks' time.

I have three weeks to put together the most perfect, brilliant, one-minute video explaining a scientific theory. The video to beat the other thousands of entries. The video that people will actually watch and understand, and think is the best.

Only three weeks. I'd better get started!

Chapter 3
A Difficult Decision

'Where's the poster?' Jazz asks me the next morning at school. She, Chloe and Zeek are all waiting for me in the yard.

I bite my lip. 'Er ... sorry. I didn't have time to do it.'

'What?' Chloe stares at me. 'I thought you said it was no problem.'

'It wasn't.' I try to explain. 'Listen – there's this competition. A really huge science one. The winner gets to go to Florida, to the Kennedy Space Center. You know – where NASA is?' I look at them excitedly.

Zeek says, 'So?'

'I have to make a video,' I say. 'For the competition. It's going to be really hard. I have to explain a scientific theory in one minute. In a way that's cool and easy to understand and people will vote for.'

My three friends are just standing and looking at me. Don't they get it?

'I spent all evening going through theories,' I say, starting to feel a bit uncomfortable. 'Trying to choose one. It needs to be quite a hard one, I think – one that most people don't understand.'

'I'll tell you what *I* don't understand,' Jazz breaks in. 'I don't understand how you've got distracted from something so important. We're raising money for the Winter Ball, remember? You signed up. You've got a job to do. Why haven't you done it?'

I look around at them all. Maybe I've said this the wrong way. 'I need to choose a theory, write a script, make props, film it, edit it and record voice-overs. It's going to take up all my spare time. I'm so sorry. I want to help, but ... I don't think I can. This prize – it's the chance of a lifetime.'

'I thought meeting On The Up was a chance of a lifetime,' Chloe says sharply.

Jazz stares at me, and when she speaks, her voice is cold. 'I can't believe you. You'd rather enter a competition you have hardly any chance of winning than help out your friends?'

She turns away. I know that she has a point. How many entries will they get? What are the chances of people watching my video and liking it enough to vote it the best?

But then I remember Suzi Klyser, the aeronautical engineer. And I bet she's not the sort of person to back away from a challenge. I bet there aren't many female aeronautical engineers either.

I look at my friends. 'I'm really sorry. This is important to me.'

There's a pause. Jazz, Chloe and Zeek look at each other. Then Jazz says, 'Fine. I guess there's nothing more to say.' And the three of them walk away, leaving me alone in the playground.

I mean the yard.

* * *

I understand why they won't talk to me for the rest of the day. I get it, I really do. I feel so bad for backing out. I'm not one to go back on my promises usually. And the Winter Ball is so important! I really want to meet On The Up.

But ... but ... science is my *life*. It's my passion: the thing I love more than anything. My mum could never afford a trip to NASA. This could be the only chance I ever get to go. My video needs to be perfect – and that means a lot of work. I can't manage another big project at the same time.

When I get home, I do some more research. There are loads of scientific theories out there, but one of the most famous ones is my favourite: Einstein's Theory of Special Relativity. It's not that hard, once you get it – but it's difficult to explain. I don't know quite how I'm going to do it, but I think I'm going to need two spaceships.

I go downstairs and knock on Mum's study door.

'Hey, sweetie,' she says, turning around in her swivel chair. 'You OK?'

'Yup,' I say. 'Have you got anything I can use to build a spaceship?'

Her eyebrows rise up her forehead. 'Are you leaving the planet?'

'No!' I laugh. 'I mean a model spaceship. Actually, I need two.'

'Two spaceships,' Mum says. 'Is this for a school project?'

'It's for a competition,' I say. 'Remember I told you about the NASA one?'

'Oh, that's right. Well, you could go through the recycling bin. There's probably something useful in there. I'm sure Gran wouldn't mind you looking through her bin either. Or Jazz's – you could pop round to her house and see what you can find there.'

'Oh. Um.' I scuff my feet on the carpet. 'Jazz isn't exactly speaking to me right now.'

'What's happened?'

I explain about the Winter Ball and On The Up and the fundraising.

'Isn't On The Up your favourite band?' Mum says, her eyes wide. 'And they're coming to your school? That's amazing!'

'It is! I'm really excited! But I can't help with the fundraising if I'm making this video.'

Mum looks at me for a moment, her head on one side. 'It's a hard choice,' she says, 'between your friends and your passion.'

'I don't like letting people down,' I admit. 'But they'll do a great job anyway.'

Mum nods, slowly. 'If you're sure ... '

I *am* sure. Of course I am. Aren't I?

Chapter 4
We're Not Friends

Over the next week, I build my two spaceships out of junk. One of them is bright and shiny with tinfoil, and a window made of see-through plastic that I got from the lid of a cake box. The other is made to look a bit tatty and rubbish. In my video, I'm going to show that time passes at different speeds depending on how fast you travel.

The shiny spaceship zooms through space at incredible speed, which makes time pass more slowly than on the ship that's not going anywhere. That's why it looks newer. Hopefully my video will explain this clearly.

In a weird way, I feel a bit like the two spaceships. The shiny one is me planning my video, writing a script, working out what I'm going to do, and being all excited about maybe zooming off to NASA to chat to brainy people. The broken-down rubbish one is me at school, where my friends won't talk to me.

I'd assumed that they'd forgive me after a bit. The day after the argument, I smiled cheerfully at Jazz when I arrived in the form room, and went to take my place next to her as usual. She stared at me and then said coldly, 'Sorry. Aria's sitting there now.'

'Excuse me,' said a voice from behind me. Aria pushed past and sat in my seat, not looking at me. I stood awkwardly, not sure what to do. Where should I sit now?

'Keisha, find a seat quickly,' said Mr Benwell.

I went to the only seat left; the one at the back next to Kyle Brooks, who smells of cheese and onion crisps and never talks to anyone.

And that's where I've sat ever since. At break times, I walk around outside by myself. If I go anywhere near Jazz, Chloe and Zeek, they turn their backs on me and walk away. Aria hangs around with them too, but she looks at me as though she feels sorry for me.

I don't want her to feel sorry for me.

At the weekend, I put the finishing touches to my spaceships. I get an email from the school saying that a list of fundraising events is now up on the school website. I click on it – and there is a poster for Jazz's hairstyling contest: the poster I should have made. It looks good. Zeek's mum is coming to judge the competition, and they're offering a free cut in her salon as a prize.

I take a breath and text Jazz:

> Saw the poster for the hairstyle contest. It looks great! Hope it goes really well and you raise loads of money ☺

She texts back almost immediately:

> Don't text me, Keisha. We're not friends. Get back to your more important project, Einstein Girl.

My stomach lurches and my eyes fill with tears. She won't forgive me for letting her down. I've messed everything up.

Chapter 5
Welcome to Science Club

In some ways, what Jazz said makes things easier. I know there isn't any point trying to be friends any more. I know I have all the time I want to work on my video and make it the best it can possibly be.

But inside I feel awful. Like someone has just reached in and pulled out my heart. Not just anyone – my best friend.

I go back to school on Monday and keep my head down. I sit next to Kyle Brooks, and try to hold my breath.

The teachers all think I'm paying lots of attention because I'm not talking to anyone. But inside my head, there's just a sad fog.

Around the school there are lots of posters advertising events by the Fundraising Committee. There's a Bake-Off competition, a fashion evening and a talent show. I overhear other kids in the class talking about Jazz's hairstyle contest. Everyone wants Nula Tsempe to be their model because of her long black hair.

It's as if I'm invisible. People don't seem to hear or see me. I hadn't realized quite how few friends I had. Jazz has been my best friend since we were little. And we made friends with Chloe and Zeek when we joined this school. There isn't really anyone else I can hang around with. I walk down the crowded corridors between lessons, feeling all alone.

'Hey! You!' a voice calls. 'You, with the blue hair thingy.'

I turn, glancing around. 'Who, me?'

A tall girl is looking at me. She must be a couple of years older. 'Are you Keisha?'

'Er ... yes.' I feel nervous.

She comes towards me. She has blond hair cut very short, and blue eyes. 'Are you the one in Kyle's class who's entering the NASA competition?'

I am taken aback. 'How did you know?'

She grins. 'Kyle told us he saw you drawing a storyboard in your file.'

'Told us? Who's *us*?'

'The Science Club,' says the girl. 'We're all entering the competition. I'm Steph. Which scientific theory are you doing for your video?'

I feel very uncomfortable. People are looking at me curiously as they go past. Suddenly I wish I were invisible again. 'Which one are *you* doing?' I ask.

Steph says, 'I'm doing the first law of thermodynamics.'

'Oh,' I say. Then I'm not sure what to say next.

'You should come along,' says Steph. 'We're meeting at lunch today. Science Lab Two.' She turns and heads off down the corridor.

'Oh,' I say again, to nobody in particular. 'Thanks.'

A poster on the wall catches my eye. 'Design a ballgown!' it says. '£2 to enter. Win a makeover for the Winter Ball!'

I press my lips together and narrow my eyes. I'd love a makeover. I'd love a ballgown. I'd love to hang out with my friends like nothing had changed. But it has. And so I'm going to Science Club.

Design a ballgown!
£2 to enter. Win a makeover for the Winter Ball!

There are three people in the lab when I get there. Steph looks up. 'Keisha!' she says. 'Come in! Welcome to Science Club!' She waves at the other two. They are boys. One of them is Kyle Brooks. He's eating a packet of cheese and onion crisps, which is totally not allowed in the science labs.

'Er ... hi,' I say, going over to the bench. 'Is this ... it?'

Steph nods. 'Yup. This is all of us. This is Sarwat, and you already know Kyle.'

Kyle glances at me but doesn't say anything.

'What's *she* doing here?' Sarwat asks Steph. He's older than me, too; probably in Steph's year.

'She's doing the NASA competition,' Steph says. 'Like us. Making a video.'

'What's she doing it on?' Sarwat asks Steph.

'*She*,' I say loudly, 'is doing Einstein's Theory of Special Relativity.'

All three of them turn to stare at me. There is a pause.

'Ohhhh-kaaaaaay,' Steph says slowly. 'That's ... kind of intense.'

Sarwat frowns. 'I bet you don't even know what that is. It's really advanced physics.'

I am annoyed. I put my bag down on the lab bench with a thump. 'I do know what it is. It's a law governing time in relation to the speed of light. The closer to the speed of light you travel, the more slowly time passes.'

There's another pause. 'Wow,' says Kyle. 'That's cool.'

I think it might be the first thing he's ever said to me.

My face goes red, though I don't know why. 'What are *you* doing?' I ask him.

'Perpetual motion,' he says, which makes me laugh, because Kyle hates sport and always tries to get out of PE.

'I've told him it doesn't count,' Steph says. 'Perpetual motion isn't a proper theory. My law of thermodynamics proves it.'

They get into an argument. I am astonished. I didn't think Kyle Brooks was interested in anything apart from cheese and onion crisps. He never puts up his hand in lessons. And now here he is – arguing about the laws of physics!

I blink, slightly stunned. Sarwat frowns at me.

'How old are you anyway?'

'Eleven,' I say.

He makes a scoffing sound. 'You really think you're going to win the competition?'

I am fed up with Sarwat's attitude. I look him straight in the eye and I say clearly, 'Yes, I do.'

Chapter 6
I'm Not Supposed to Talk to You

Sitting next to Kyle Brooks that afternoon in registration feels different. I mean, he's gone back to not talking to me, but now I know there's a lot more to him than I realized. You'd never know, looking at him, that he was a science nerd. I wouldn't have thought he was a nerd at all, actually. If I'm perfectly honest – and I'm a bit ashamed about this now – I thought he was kind of ... boring.

In Science the next day, we're doing heat expansion of metal. The teacher asks a question, and I see Kyle write down the answer in his scrawling handwriting. But he doesn't put up his hand. Someone near the front answers the question and gets it wrong.

The teacher says, 'Come on! Anyone else?' But Kyle doesn't say anything.

The teacher sighs and gives us the answer – the same one that Kyle has scribbled down.

'Why didn't you put your hand up?' I whisper to him. 'You knew that.'

He scowls at me and puts his hand over his work so I can't see anything else he writes.

* * *

'How's the video going?' Mum asks when I get home from school.

'All right,' I say. 'I've built my two spaceships, but I've got no one to pilot them.'

She puts her head on one side, thinking. 'How big do the pilots need to be?'

I hold my hands apart. 'About that big. And I don't want to use some stupid teddy bear.'

'What about one of your old dolls?' asks Mum. 'You know – the ones with impossible feet that won't stand up.'

I stare at her, incredulous. *'Them?'* I say. 'But they're … well. They're for fashion.'

Mum gives me a look. 'Are you suggesting that just because they're blonde and glamorous they can't pilot a spaceship?'

I open my mouth and close it again. She's
right of course. Just because a doll comes with
ballgowns and cute puppies, it doesn't mean she's
not smart. I mean – I like ballgowns *and* physics.

I grin at Mum. 'Good idea.'

And so, two of my old dolls are kitted out in
tin foil spacesuits and fixed into the spaceships.

The thing that's going to be hardest about this
video is showing the path of light. Light moves

too quickly for the naked eye to see, which means that using actual light in the video will be no help at all in explaining the theory.

I fall asleep pondering the difficulty of light representation in my video.

In the night, I have a dream. I am walking down the corridor, and every classroom door is open. Inside each room, a club is meeting, and a person stands in the doorway calling to me.

'Keisha! Hey, Keisha, come and join our club!'
'No – ours is the best!' 'Keisha, you promised to be in our club!'

In the dream, the noise from people shouting starts to frighten me. The people in the doorways lean out, their faces distorting and their mouths huge, almost trying to swallow me up. Kyle Brooks is there too, improbably holding a pair of knitting needles and pleading with me to join his knitting club.

I panic and run – but my legs move impossibly slowly. And then I look down and realize that Kyle's wool has tangled around my legs and the faster I try to run, the tighter it pulls, until I am trussed up like a chicken. I trip and fall, squirming desperately in an attempt to get myself free.

And then I wake up. And I know how to represent light in my video.

'Mum!' I call. 'Have you got any wool?'

* * *

At school, I am getting used to being invisible. My friends – my ex-friends, I should say – don't even acknowledge me. I have given up saying hello to them – they never reply.

I've given up taking part in lessons too. What's the point? If the teacher praises me, I don't feel happy. I'm also afraid that if I get something wrong, everyone will laugh at me. So Kyle and I sit together, hardly speaking to each other or to anyone else. It's kind of comforting though, to have him there.

About a week before the competition deadline, I accidentally bump into Aria in the corridor. 'Oh, sorry!' she says, before seeing it's me and turning bright red. 'Got to go.'

I can't help myself. I blurt out, 'Please stay.'

She stops and looks around nervously. Then she leans forward and says in a whisper, 'Look, Keisha, I'm not being mean, but I'm not supposed to talk to you.'

Tears spring to my eyes. 'But it *is* being mean,'

I say. 'I know I let everyone down, but I don't deserve this.'

'Sorry,' says Aria. 'I'm not the one making the rules.' She hurries away.

I am late to Science Club. Not that the others notice. They're all crowded round Sarwat's laptop, sneering at something.

'What are you watching?' I ask, putting down my bag and coming round to see.

'The first few competition videos are up,' says Steph, not taking her eyes off the screen. 'And they are *really* bad. No way is anyone going to vote for them!'

'There's one with a girl in a tree, pretending to be an apple,' says Kyle with a snort. 'It's like some awful drama piece.'

'She falls out of the tree!' Sarwat explains, bursting into laughter. 'And then lies on the grass explaining gravity! It's just embarrassing.' He scrolls through the other videos, and my heart sinks. There are so many already! And we still have a week before the deadline! How many entries will there be when the competition closes? What chance do I have?

'I'm posting mine tomorrow,' says Steph, sounding proud. 'It's dead good.'

'You've finished?' says Sarwat, impressed.

'Yup. I'm so going to win.'

'You done yours yet?' Kyle asks me.

'I've done most of the filming,' I tell him. 'Got to record the voice-overs, and the editing will take ages. I've got over two minutes' worth of material. Don't know how I'm going to get it down to one minute.'

'Good luck with that,' says Sarwat sarcastically. 'Maybe you should have picked something easier!'

I glare at him. 'I can do it.'

As I leave the lab, I feel determined and strong. I *can* do this!

Then my phone beeps with a text from Jazz:

Don't try to make friends with any of us. We only want REAL friends.

My hands tremble. I only wanted to talk to Aria! Why is Jazz still being so horrible? I stuff the phone back in my bag and head to class. I should go back to keeping my head down.

But that afternoon, the whispering begins.

Chapter 7
Time to Change

I don't notice it to start with. I'm busy writing down the information on the board and listening to the English teacher droning on about metaphors. And then I hear a stifled giggle directly behind me, and I am suddenly alert. As I put down my pen, I glance to my left. Two pairs of eyes immediately flick away.

I glance to my right. No one is looking at me. But Shanice, at the next table, is staring very hard at her exercise book and smirking.

The teacher turns. 'Shanice, is there something the matter?'

Shanice shakes her head, but her shoulders are still trembling with laughter. 'No, Miss.'

Kyle isn't in English with me, and I almost miss his solid silent presence.

Tears fill my eyes, and I don't look round any more. It would only make things worse and set off another sequence of sniggers. Instead,

I do what I have learned to do recently: make no sudden movements, catch no one's eye, behave as though I don't deserve to be there.

When the lesson ends, I make sure I'm the last person to leave the room. Someone bumps into me as they go past, and I feel a hand on my back.

My blood runs cold. Is there something on my back? Has someone stuck a note on to me? I reach round but can't feel anything. Panicking, I head out into the corridor, and to my relief I see Kyle up ahead. He's turning away from his locker, but I plan my route through the moving bodies and intercept him at the corner. 'Kyle,' I say, 'please help me. Do I have something on my back?' I swing round.

'No,' he says.

'Are you sure?'

'There's nothing there.' He pops open a packet of crisps and digs his fingers into it.

The smell of synthetic cheese reaches my nostrils and I grimace.

'Oh. Thanks for looking.'

He nods at me and heads off.

It occurs to me then that if, back in the old days, I'd asked Jazz if there was something on my back, I'd have got the third-degree from her. What did I think was there? Why did I think it? What led up to this suspicion? Had I annoyed someone in the class? We'd have sat down and  made a list of possible suspects. Then she'd have given me a consoling hug and suggested we go and eat chocolate or something.

Kyle didn't offer any of that, because he didn't see anything odd in my asking him. I guess that means that to him, unkind notes stuck on backs are the norm. You just shrug them off. I wonder how many notes have been stuck to *his* back over the years.

That's really sad. Poor Kyle.

* * *

When school ends, I go out with everyone else into the yard. Jazz is there at the school gates, talking and laughing with Chloe.

Something inside me feels hot and angry, so I go up to her. 'Hey,' I say. 'We need to talk.'

She glances at me and her expression hardens. 'I've got nothing to say to you.'

'Well, I've got something to say to *you*,' I tell her. 'It's not fair, what you're doing. I know I let you down. I *said* I'm sorry. But this video is really important to me. You know I love science. It's what I want to do with my life.

You should be more supportive to me. I thought we were friends.'

'Friends!' Jazz takes a step towards me. 'How dare you! We've been friends for years, and yet when it came to doing something for yourself or something for your mates, you turned your back on us! You're *selfish*, Keisha. You expect everyone else to do the fundraising for you, and you can just enjoy the results. I'm not wasting my time talking to you. I've got stuff to do, with my *real* friends.'

Jazz links arms with Chloe, and the two of them stalk off.

I stare after them until they've turned the corner and disappeared.

Am I selfish? Is it selfish to want to follow your dreams? Maybe Jazz is right.

Maybe she's not.

Either way, I realize it doesn't matter. I don't want to feel like this any more. I don't want to be invisible.

I want my friends back.
And there's only one way to do it.

Chapter 8
Back in the Group

The Fundraising Committee meets the very next lunchtime, in the same room where it all started. My stomach is fluttery with nerves, but I walk straight up to Jazz, Chloe and Zeek, and say, 'I'm so sorry about what I did. I never meant to let you down. I'm giving up on the science competition; I want to help raise money for the ball instead. I'll work afternoons and weekends – whatever it takes.'

There is a stunned silence. Everyone is staring at me – I can feel it. I keep my eyes fixed on Jazz. This is the moment. This is the calculated risk. Win or lose – right here, right now.

Jazz stares at me, our eyes locked. Hers narrow. 'All right,' she says slowly. 'It's our hairstyling contest this afternoon, so you can help with that. You need to stay on after school until six o'clock.'

'Oh,' I say. 'Oh – six o'clock?'

'Is that a problem?' Jazz's tone sharpens.

'No,' I say hastily. 'No, not at all.'

'All right then,' says Jazz. 'But don't expect things to be the way they used to be.'

I blink quickly because I'm afraid I might cry. 'Of course not,' I say. Then I sit down next to them and ask, 'So, what do you want me to do this afternoon?'

Everyone around us loses interest and goes back to discussing and planning.

It's a test, I know. But if I can pass, I'll be back in the group. It's worth the risk.

* * *

Mum is confused when I ring to say I'm staying on at school to help with the event. 'But I thought you wanted to finish your video? Isn't it the deadline in a couple of days?'

'I've decided not to enter,' I say. 'My friends are more important.'

She is silent for a moment, and then she says, 'Keisha, you know I'm so proud of you for your achievements. You're a clever girl. Friends *are* important. But don't lose yourself by trying to please others. OK?'

'OK,' I say.

'I'll pick you up at half past six, all right?' Mum pauses and then says, 'Can I ask why you changed your mind?'

I haven't told her what's been going on at school. She might have wanted to get involved and make a fuss. 'I just realized I'd made the wrong decision,' I say. 'I was letting them down.'

'Sounds to me,' says Mum, before hanging up, 'like they've been letting *you* down.'

* * *

Loads of people come along to the hairstyle competition! I stand on the door and take the money as people come in – you have to pay to take part, and we have a lot of entries. The money tray gets heavier and heavier.

I think Jazz and the others are surprised by how many people come, too. It takes ages to get everyone organized, because we haven't set out enough chairs, and things have to be hastily

moved round. Zeek's mum is there, wafting perfume and swishing her own incredible hair, as though it can somehow inspire everyone around her to greater heights.

Everyone who's entered has one hour to work on their model's hair. That allows time to do really intricate designs, like plaits and twists and all sorts. Before long, the hall is filled with the smell of hairspray, and my head spins.

I pick up a bottle of spray and stare at the ingredients on the back. It's an incredible list of chemicals – ethylhexyl methoxycinnamate, aminomethyl propanol, benzyl benzoate – and I wonder who invented or discovered these particular combinations of molecules and their hair-controlling possibilities. What do their chemical bonds look like?

'Keisha! Are you *here*, or what?' It's Chloe's voice snapping at me.

I blink and turn, hastily putting down the hairspray. 'I'm here! Sorry! What do you want me to do?'

'Get a broom. Samuel has spilled a whole pot of glitter on the floor.'

I rush to sort it out.

Suddenly, the hour is up, and I look round to see a parade of incredible hairstyles. A girl I don't know has spent the entire hour plaiting her friend's hair and then spraying each plait a different colour, so it looks like a head of rainbows. Someone else has put enough gel in their model's hair to make it stiff like concrete, and spiked it like a dandelion clock.

Nula Tsempe's hair has been wound around her head like one of those soft ice creams you buy from vans, and is festooned with white flowers. She looks stunning.

Zeek's mum is clearly impressed and takes a very long time to decide the winner. I keep glancing at the clock on the wall. Once the contest is over, there's going to be a whole load of clearing up to do, and it's quarter past six already. Mum will be setting off to pick me up soon, and I don't think we'll be finished.

I sidle up to Aria, who's been helping too, and I say, 'What time do you think we'll finish?'

She shrugs. 'I dunno. Doesn't everyone look amazing?'

'Yeah,' I say, wondering if I can slip out. But Jazz would notice. And Chloe and Zeek. I can't risk offending them again. They wouldn't take me back a second time, I'm sure. So I take my phone out of my pocket and quickly text Mum:

Sorry, event running late. Can you pick me up at 7 pm instead?

It's gone seven o'clock by the time I get out of school, and Mum's face as I get into the car is cross. She says, 'Keisha, this is not on.'

I burst into tears.

Chapter 9
A Bitter Blow

My mum is brilliant. She listens to all of it – about my friends being horrible, and the text messages, and my decision to give up the competition because of what they said – and she doesn't tell me off. Instead, she sighs and gives me a hug, and says, 'I wish you'd told me.'

'I was afraid you'd go into school,' I say, wiping my eyes and blowing my nose for about the seventh time. 'And make a big fuss – and then things would get even worse.'

Mum rolls her eyes. 'You have no faith in me!' she complains. 'Do you really think I'd go crashing around like some clumsy ogre, making your life difficult?'

I smile in shaky relief. 'No, I guess not. Sorry.'

'What are you doing about it, then?' asks Mum.

I shrug. 'Whatever they tell me to. I have to, if I want to stay friends with them.'

Mum says nothing for a long moment, and then she says, 'Keisha, I don't know everything. Friends are really important, but some friends are better than others. I hope these ones are worth it.'

I look down at the crumpled tissues in my hand and say, 'I'm sure they are.'

* * *

It's the day of the deadline for the science competition and, as I walk to school, I can't help but feel a bit of a pang. My video is so nearly finished – and it's good, I know it is. But between helping out at the hairstyle contest and making sure I'm available for my friends, not to mention my homework, I haven't had time to do it. Which is fine, because I've made my decision. I'm listening to a new podcast about quantum mechanics, which is the study of energy and molecules on a very small scale. I'm not sure I understand it very well, but that's partly because I'm distracted by feeling a bit sad.

Still, I cheer up when I see my friends in the yard. Jazz, Chloe and Zeek are there, along with Aria, who's still part of the group even though she's kind of quiet. I call out to them as I approach, and they turn to smile at me. 'Keisha!' says Jazz. 'Guess how much money we made from our hairstyle competition?'

'Two hundred and forty-five pounds!' squeaks Chloe, excited.

'Wow!' I say. 'That's amazing!'

'The Fundraising Committee is going to be so impressed,' Jazz says, grinning at me.

'We think we might have raised the most money out of all the events – and that means we get to meet On The Up face-to-face!'

I feel myself smile my biggest smile ever. It has all been worth it! I totally made the right decision.

At lunchtime, we all go to the committee meeting. Jazz takes my arm as we head down the corridor and I feel as if I'm walking on air. Who cares about science competitions? I'm going to meet On The Up!

But Jessica, the Chair of the committee, looks serious. 'Settle down!' she shouts over the excited noise. 'We've got something to tell you.'

Instantly, there's a hush. Fear grips us all. Has On The Up pulled out? Is one of them sick?

'You've all been doing amazing work,' Jessica begins. 'So many great events, and so much money raised. Even just the other day – another two hundred pounds from the hairstyle competition.'

'Two hundred and forty-five,' mutters Chloe.

'You've raised an incredible amount of money,' says Jessica, consulting a piece of paper. 'As of today, our total stands at two thousand, one hundred and eleven pounds.' She looks up at everyone. 'But I'm afraid there's bad news. Mr Hanover says the band needs the money one month in advance, or they can't keep the booking. And that's today, and ... we haven't got enough. I'm so sorry, everyone.'

There is a stunned, sickened silence.

'Mr Hanover has promised that the event will still go ahead,' Jessica continues, desperately. 'He says it's too late to book another band, but we can have a DJ. Mr Proctor DJs in his spare time, apparently ... ' She trails off, wilting under the disgusted noises that greet this suggestion.

Jazz turns to look at me, and I see my own despair in her eyes. 'All of that ... and we didn't make it.'

I don't think it occurred to any of us that we might not be able to raise the money. We just assumed we would. And that On The Up would be coming here, to our little school, to play the most amazing concert of our lives. That we would get to meet them, and have our photos taken.

And now it's all over.

And a tiny voice inside my head says: *You gave up the science competition to help out, and now you've failed at this too.*

* * *

Messages fly thick and fast that evening. Jazz is furious that Mr Hanover didn't say at the beginning that there was a deadline for the money. Zeek can't stop whingeing about Mr Proctor and how he plays 'old people's music', and how the Winter Ball is going to be terrible and not worth going to. Chloe just keeps sending crying faces.

Then Jazz texts:

> I just asked my dad for a loan. He laughed and said there would be no guarantee of getting the money back.

Chloe:

> We need to win the lottery.

Then my phone makes a different text-alert sound.

It's Steph, from Science Club:

> Did you get your video in? Hardly anyone else has done thermodynamics, so I reckon I'm in with a great chance of winning that trip and the money!

I stare at her text, frozen to the spot. Money? What money? I don't remember anything about money. I was so focused on the chance to win the trip to NASA, I'm not sure I even read the small print ...

With trembling fingers, I boot up the laptop and go to the competition website. There are *hundreds* of videos online now! Heart thudding, I click through to the Terms and Conditions.

Oh. Oh my. As well as the trip to the Kennedy Space Center, the winner gets a thousand pounds for their school.

A thousand pounds. Enough to make up the rest of what we need for the Winter Ball ...

Hitting all the wrong keys on my phone, I tap out a text to everyone:

> If only I'd entered the science comp. The winner gets £1000 for their school!

There is a pause, and then Jazz, Chloe, Zeek and Aria all text me at the same time:

> WHAT? ENTER IT RIGHT NOW!

The deadline is midnight tonight. It's already eight o'clock. I still have so much to do to my video. Can I finish it in time?

* * *

Mum stares at me like I'm mad. 'You want to stay up till midnight finishing the science video that you decided not to finish because your friends were more important, but now your friends *want* you to finish it because they want the prize money for the Winter Ball?'

I nod. 'That's exactly it!'

She gives a kind of laugh. 'I wish someone had explained to me just how complicated being a mum would be. Every time I think I've got it figured out, the rules change!'

'So, can I?' I ask impatiently, itching to get back to my room.

She looks at me. 'Can I stop you?'

'No!' I say, and turn and run.

I load up my video-editing software and open the file. Then I get to work.

At some point, Mum brings me a drink and a biscuit and tells me it's eleven o'clock. I mumble something, and ignore the drink and the biscuit. I don't know if I'm going to make it. It's going to be so close!

At half past eleven, my video is finished. It's got everything I wanted it to have, and I'm proud of it. I am weak with relief as I log into the site and select 'Upload'.

Thank you. File size 60.4MB. Upload time remaining 29 mins . . .

'What?' I gasp at the screen. Twenty-nine minutes! I glance at the clock. It's 11.31 pm!

How can it take that long to upload a video? I suppose there must be lots of people out there who've left it to the last minute, slowing down the site. But if it takes that long ... I still might not make the midnight deadline!

The next twenty-nine minutes are the longest of my life. I daren't leave the computer in case something goes wrong halfway through and I have to try to start the upload again. Not that I would have time for that! If it goes wrong, that's it – I'm doomed.

I watch the progress bar as it slowly turns green from one end to the other and I feel like the whole responsibility for the Winter Ball is resting on my shoulders. Even if I get my video accepted, the only way I'll win is if enough people vote for it. I could have done all this for nothing; have my hopes dashed all over again, and worse – this time, taking everyone else's hopes with me.

11.58 pm:

Upload time remaining 1 minute . . .

I realize I have bitten four of my nails while waiting. I sit on my hands to avoid biting any more.

11.59 pm:

> Congratulations! Your video has been successfully uploaded. You can share it using the link below.

I email my friends:

```
I made it! Here's the link!
```

As I send the message, I let out the biggest sigh ever. I've done it. It's in; it's gone. I've entered. And now there is nothing more I can do.

So I eat my biscuit and go to bed.

Chapter 10
I Want to Say Sorry

The next morning, I can barely keep my eyes open. Jazz throws her arms around me in the playground. 'You did it! Keisha, your video is AMAZING! You're a total genius!'

'I am?' I say, bewildered. 'You watched it?'

'Of *course* I watched it! I watched it, like, *four* times in a row. You make it all sound so easy, Keisha! I told my dad all about it, and he was

really impressed I understood it. I bet I could explain Einstein's Theory of Special Relativity to anyone now!'

Jazz is practically bouncing around the yard.

'Oh, wow.' I am filled with happiness.

Jazz stops bouncing for a moment and says, 'Keisha, listen. I want to say sorry. I've been really awful to you.'

'Oh, no – ' I say uncomfortably. 'It's OK.'

'I was so gutted when you walked out on us,' Jazz goes on. 'I couldn't believe it. It felt like you were turning your back on me. All those times we'd sung along to On The Up in your bedroom, made up stupid games about them … I felt like you were stamping all over those memories. But I know how much you love your science stuff. Geek.' She smiles and gives me a gentle shove. 'I should have been more understanding. I took it all too far. Maybe it's because I wish I had a brain like yours. You're so clever. I'm rubbish at everything.'

'Don't be silly!' I exclaim. 'You're really good at organizing things – look at the hairstyle contest! Think how much money you made!' I give her a little shove back. 'Yeah, you were horrid. But I get it, and I'm sorry I didn't handle stuff better either.'

Jazz links her arm through mine as we head into school. 'I'm going to tell everyone about my friend the science genius. And get them to vote for your video.'

'Because then we can have the money for the Winter Ball,' I say.

'Because it's the *best*,' says Jazz firmly. 'Honestly, Keisha, it's the coolest. And we're going straight to Mr Hanover's room right now to get him to give us another week to raise the money.'

* * *

The Head won't listen to start with. 'It's not my rule,' he insists. 'It's the band's. It's in the contract. We don't have enough money, so they don't have to honour the contract.'

'Sir,' says Jazz firmly, 'Keisha's going to win this competition. You just watch her video.'

Mr Hanover sits very still while the video plays, and then he looks at me. 'You made this?'

'Yes,' I say, red-faced.

'It's very, very good. Did you get help from one of the Science teachers?'

'No,' I say. 'I did it on my own.'

'Well,' he says, staring at me as though he's never noticed me before (which, to be fair, he possibly hasn't – this is a big school). 'Well then, I'm impressed. And I'm going to get on the phone to the band's manager right now, to ask him for an extension. Just in case you win.'

'Oh, wow,' I say, in a strangled voice.

Mr Hanover continues: 'We should run a campaign to get people to vote for it.'

'I'm on it, sir,' says Jazz.

She's as good as her word. By the end of the day, the walls of the corridors are covered in brightly coloured posters with a picture of me and a link to my video, and a demand to vote for it.

Students start glancing at me in a puzzled way as I walk to my lessons. Whereas before I would have felt miserable and kept my head down, now I feel proud. Jazz walks with me, saying loudly to people, 'This is her! This is Keisha, and you have to vote for her amazing video.'

'Why should we?' calls out a boy.

Jazz turns on him. 'Because it's awesome! *And* because if she wins, we get to have On The Up at the Winter Ball.'

I love that she mentioned winning the money second.

The next week passes in a whirlwind. Everyone at school now knows who I am. People stop me in the corridor to exclaim how they understand advanced physics because of me. Most incredibly, one of the band members from On The Up puts a message about it on a social media site! Suddenly, my video is going viral! 'Vote for this kid!' says Ranj from the band. 'Only eleven but already as brainy as Einstein! She makes science cool!' I nearly faint from excitement.

I watch some of the other videos too, including those from the other Science Club members. Well – not Kyle, because he never managed to sort out how to explain perpetual motion, but Steph's and Sarwat's videos aren't bad at all. At Science Club though, they both admit they voted for mine.

'Pretty good,' says Steph, slightly reluctantly, I feel.

'It's better than most of the rubbish on there,' agrees Sarwat.

'Thanks,' I say, trying not to look too pleased.

Kyle doesn't say anything until we're heading back to class. Then he says, 'I'm glad everything worked out with your friends.'

I feel a sort of pang in my chest. Since I decided to go back to my friends, Kyle has been sitting alone again. What's kind of sad is that he doesn't seem to mind. As though people come and go, and nothing ever changes. We weren't actually friends, but I feel bad anyway. So the next day, I buy a packet of cheese and onion crisps and leave them on his desk. I don't know if he knows they're from me, but he smiles when he sees them.

On the day the voting closes, the school has a special assembly about Albert Einstein and they show my video. I cringe at seeing myself up there, along with two dolls glued into home-made spaceships. The wool that I borrowed from Mum is stretched across our garden hedge in zigzags, representing light beams bouncing inside each spaceship. One length of wool has short tight zigzags whilst the other (the faster one) has long stretched-out zigzags.

In the video, I gather up the wool to show how the path is longer for the light beam in the faster spaceship. But since we know light speed is a constant, then *time* must be the thing that is different in the two spaceships. For the spaceship that is travelling nearly at the speed of light, time is passing more slowly than in the spaceship that's staying still. Poor shabby doll will age faster than glossy speedy doll.

When the video finishes, there's a spontaneous outburst of applause. 'Whatever the outcome of the competition tomorrow,' Mr Hanover tells everyone, 'we are all very proud of Keisha. She has taken her particular talent to a very high level, and is an inspiration to us all.'

Gosh. I'm hot all over with embarrassment.

When I get home, I load the web page for the competition. At the moment, my video is in the top five for public votes. But when the clock hits midnight, the final results will be kept secret until eight o'clock tomorrow morning. I go to bed, but my stomach is flipping around like a dying fish and I can't get comfortable. Everyone is counting on me.

I stare at the ceiling with burning eyes, and wait for the morning.

Chapter 11
Geeks Can Dance!

I sleep through my alarm because I only fell asleep at 3 am. Mum comes to wake me, shaking me gently. 'Keisha, sweetie, it's morning. You really must get up. You'll be late.'

My eyes ping open like the lids are elastic. The competition! 'Is it eight o'clock?' I gasp at Mum, making her jump.

'Ten to,' she says. 'You've got ten minutes to get dressed before the outcome of the world is announced.' She smiles, but I know she realizes how much this competition means to me.

I hug her very hard. 'Thank you,' I say into her shoulder, all muffled. 'Thanks for being such a brilliant mum.'

'Oh.' Her arms tighten around me. 'That's ... what a lovely thing to say. Thank *you* for being a brilliant daughter. I'm so proud of you, every day. Sometimes I feel you've missed out on not having a dad around – '

I shake my head. 'He left. You're all I need.'

She sniffs and wipes her eyes, and then says, 'You'd better get up! Eight minutes until the announcement!'

Eight minutes can feel like eight days sometimes. Mum puts toast in front of me, but I can't eat it. She lets me use her computer because it's faster than my old laptop. I refresh the screen over and over again. Eight o'clock comes and goes, and the website stays the same.

8.02 … still no news.

My phone beeps with a text from Jazz:

> WHAT'S GOING ON WITH THIS SITE???

I smile tightly and wonder just how many kids from our school are glued to this website this morning, unable to eat because they're so nervous.

8.04 … no change.

8.05 …

OH.

OH, MY GOOD GOLLY GOSHNESS.

SCIENCE THEORY COMPETITION: WINNER – KEISHA COOPER!

I try to call for Mum, but my throat has closed up and only a strangled noise comes out. I stare at the screen, unable to believe it. My phone beeps – once, twice, three times, four times … but I don't pick it up. I can't move.

I won. I actually won.

On The Up is coming to play at our Winter Ball. I'll get to meet them. My friends think I'm brilliant.

And … and I get to go to NASA.

I think I might faint.

* * *

Three weeks later, I am standing at the school gates in the dark, shivering in a floor-length blue satin dress. Beside me, Jazz whoops with excitement, resplendent in a pale pink dress with sequinned bodice and puffy skirt. The others are there too: Zeek, looking extremely stylish in a purple suit; Chloe, in a kind of floral

fishtail frock (shiny gel nails covering up the bitten ones); and Aria, in shimmering green like some kind of wood nymph. We look at each other, smiling. The Winter Ball is finally here, and so is On The Up. The first notes of their hit song ring out from the school building, and all five of us scream in excitement, link arms and rush through the gates.

'You're the best, Keisha,' Jazz says to me, giving my hand a squeeze.

I'm about to reply, and then I see Kyle come through the gates behind us. About a week before, we were at Science Club, and I was talking about the Ball. 'I'm not going,' Kyle said. 'Geeks like studying. We can't dance.'

'What are you talking about?' I replied. 'Who says we can't do both?'

He'd just shrugged and turned away, so I'm really surprised to see him here tonight. He looks quite nice in a suit, and for once he doesn't have a packet of crisps in his hand.

He's on his own though, and that doesn't
seem right.

I make a decision. 'Go on ahead,' I say to Jazz.
'I'm going to walk in with Kyle.'

She stares at me. 'What? But ... oh, all right,
then. See you in there. Don't hang about – we
get to meet the band in only an hour!' She and
the others run into the school.

An hour, I think, as I watch Kyle head towards me. It's not long to wait, unless you're travelling at the speed of light. Good thing humans can't do that. Though maybe, when I'm grown-up, I could figure it out ...